COVER: "THE STORM ON THE SEA OF GALILEE" IS AN EARLY REMBRANDT PAINTING THAT TELLS THE STORY OF MAN'S ETERNAL STRUGGLE WITH NATURE AND WITH HIMSELF. THE ARTIST HAS GIVEN A HIGH SENSE OF CONFLICT AND HAS HEIGHTENED THE EXCITEMENT WITH SHARP SPLASHES OF COLOR AND DRAMATIC FORM.

STUDY OF TWO BIRDS OF PARADISE, LOUVRE, PARIS

OLD MAN WITH RED HAT   STAATLICHE MUSEUM, BERLIN (WEST)

DEDICATED TO JOACHIM PROBST, AN UNRECOGNIZED
AMERICAN MASTER

WORLD RIGHTS RESERVED BY ERNEST RABOFF AND GEMINI SMITH, INC.   ISBN Trade: 0-385-07942-7
Library: 0-385-02402-9
LIBRARY OF CONGRESS CATALOGUE CARD NO. 70-121782   PRINTED IN JAPAN BY TOPPAN

HARMENSZ. VAN RIJN
REMBRANDT

By Ernest Raboff

ART
FOR
CHILDREN

A GEMINI SMITH BOOK

EDITED BY BRADLEY SMITH

PUBLISHED BY
DOUBLEDAY & CO., INC.

GARDEN CITY, NEW YORK

HARMENSZ. VAN RIJN REMBRANDT

WAS BORN IN LEIDEN, HOLLAND, ON JULY 15, 1606.
HE DIED IN THE CITY OF AMSTERDAM IN OCTOBER OF 1669.

HIS FATHER, HARMEN, WAS A MILLER. HIS MOTHER,
CORNELIA, WAS *THE DAUGHTER OF A BAKER. THEIR ARTIST
SON WAS THE EIGHTH OF NINE CHILDREN. HE BEGAN HIS
PAINTING STUDIES AT 15 YEARS OF AGE. AT THE AGE OF 25
HE WAS ESTABLISHED PROFESSIONALLY IN AMSTERDAM.
IN A FEW YEARS, YOUNG REMBRANDT WAS VERY SUCCESS-
FUL AND WAS RECOGNIZED AS AN IMPORTANT ARTIST.

REMBRANDT'S FIRST WIFE, SASKIA, MOTHER OF HIS
SON TITUS, DIED AFTER 10 YEARS OF MARRIAGE. HIS SECOND
WIFE, HENDRICKJE, WAS THE MOTHER OF HIS DAUGHTER CORNELIA.

THIS ARTIST'S REMARKABLE, CONSTANT FAME IS EQUALED
BY ONLY A FEW OLD MASTERS.
THE LINES, FORMS, AND COLORS
OF HIS PORTRAITS WILL REMAIN
TRUE TO LIFE FOREVER. TOWARD
THE END OF HIS CAREER, COLOR
LIKE SUNLIGHT FLOWED FROM
REMBRANDT'S BRUSH ONTO
HIS CANVAS AND CREATED
IMPRESSIONISM HUNDREDS OF
YEARS BEFORE TURNER, MONET.
AND RENOIR WERE BORN.

PORTRAIT OF REMBRANDT BY RABOFF

REMBRANDT HAS LEFT US ALL OF HIS MEMORIES IN DRAWINGS AND IN STROKES OF GLOWING PAINT, NOT WORDS. THEY ARE HIS POEMS, HIS PHILOSOPHY.

LIFE IS WHATEVER ONE SEES.

REMBRANDT SAW THE BEAUTIFUL IN EVERYTHING FROM A LION TO A CHILD, A LANDSCAPE TO A HELMET, AN OLD WOMAN'S FACE TO THE WRINKLED ROOT OF A TREE.

HE LOVED ART AND ALL THINGS CREATED BY MANKIND WITH WELL-TRAINED HANDS.

HE LOVED NATURE. DOGS, ELEPHANTS, FLOWERS, BIRDS, AND ABOVE ALL ELSE MOTHERS AND CHILDREN.

REMBRANDT KNEW IF HE PAINTED WHAT HE SAW HIS WORK WOULD BE TRUTHFUL. IF HE PAINTED WITH LOVE HIS WORK WOULD BE GOOD. IF HIS ART WERE TRUTHFUL AND GOOD, IT WOULD BE BEAUTIFUL.

REMBRANDT KNEW THAT IT WAS LOVE THAT GAVE MEANING TO HIS WORK AND TO HIS LIFE.

SELF PORTRAIT, ETCHING   RIJKSMUSEUM, AMSTERDAM

REMBRANDT PAINTED THIS SELF-PORTRAIT WHEN HE WAS 23 YEARS OLD. ONLY EIGHT YEARS AFTER HE HAD BEGUN HIS STUDIES AT AGE 15, HE WAS A MASTER.

REMBRANDT WAS A PORTRAIT PAINTER. EVERY FACE HE PAINTED REVEALS TWO SIDES OF THE SITTER'S PERSONALITY.

HE LIGHTED ONE SIDE OF THE FACE TO SHOW A PERSON AS OTHERS IN THE WORLD MIGHT SEE THE FEATURES. HIDDEN IN SHADOWS ON THE OTHER SIDE WERE SENSITIVITIES, DREAMS, QUESTIONS, AND AMBITIONS.

COVER ONE HALF OF THIS SELF-PORTRAIT OF THE ARTIST AS A YOUNG MAN AND SEE REMBRANDT AS HE APPEARED TO BE IN THE LIGHT OF DAY. THEN DO THE SAME TO THE OTHER SIDE TO SEE HIM AS HE SAW HIMSELF.

A SAILING BOAT ON THE NIEWE MEER   DEVONSHIRE COLLECTION, CHATSWORTH, PERMISSION OF CHATSWORTH SETTLEMENT TRUSTEES

SELF PORTRAIT, 1629   ROYAL PICTURE GALLERY   MAURITSHUIS, THE HAGUE

REMBRANDT'S MOTHER

HAS A BEAUTIFUL FACE, LINED AND WRINKLED BY THE LOVING CARE, HARD WORK, AND THE LONG YEARS DEVOTED TO HER HUSBAND AND NINE CHILDREN.

MOTHER OF REMBRANDT   RIJKS MUSEUM, AMSTERDAM

THE BOWED **HEAD** AND BENT **SHOULDERS** UNDER THE WARM SHAWL AND FUR-LINED CLOAK ARE SUPPORTED BY THE STURDY HANDS DRAPED AROUND THE TOP OF HER CANE.

CORNELIA VAN RIJN'S EYES, WATERY AND RED-RIMMED, STILL SPARKLE WITH LIFE. THEY

SEEM TO BE LIGHTED WITH PRIDE AND WITH LOVE FOR THIS FAMOUS SON OF HERS WHO IS

PAINTING

HER

PORTRAIT

PORTRAIT OF BOY IN PROFILE   BRITISH MUSEUM

REMBRANDT'S MOTHER   KUNSTHISTORISCHES MUSEUM, VIENNA

"HARMEN VAN RIJN", REMBRANDT'S FATHER, WAS A MILLER IN THE DUTCH VILLAGE OF RIJN.

HE WAS A CRAFTSMAN AT HIS TRADE OF GRINDING WHEAT INTO PURE AND FINE FLOUR FOR BREAD.

HARMEN ENCOURAGED HIS SON IN HIS DESIRE TO PAINT.

IN REMBRANDT'S EYES HIS FATHER WAS A STRONG AND NOBLE MAN.

BEGGAR LEANING ON A STICK
THE METROPOLITAN MUSEUM OF ART, N.Y., HARRIS BRISBANE DICK FUND

THIS ARTIST, WHO COLLECTED AND LOVED FINE CLOTHING AND BEAUTIFUL ORNAMENTS, PAINTED HIS FATHER IN THE FEATHERED HAT, METAL NECK PLATE, NECKLACE, AND VELVET ROBE OF A DUTCH GENTLEMAN.

REMBRANDT'S FATHER   THE ART INSTITUTE OF CHICAGO, MR. AND MRS. W. W. KIMBALL COLLECTION

THE OMVAL, 1645   METROPOLITAN MUSEUM OF ART, H.O.HAVEMEYER COLLECTION, NEW YORK

THE EQUESTRIAN PORTRAIT

SPARKLES LIKE A FIRE.

GOLD, WHITE, BROWN, RED, AND BLUE FORM FLAMES OF BURNING COLOR.

THE HANDSOME GRAY HORSE REARS UPWARD HOLDING HIS FRONT LEGS LIKE A PAIR OF TONGS.

THE RIDER'S PROUD FACE SHOWS HE IS AWARE OF THE EXCITING FIGURE HE MAKES ON HIS MAGNIFICENT MOUNT.

THE ANIMAL'S WHITE MANE IS CURLED TO MATCH THE HORSEMAN'S LONG, SHOULDER-LENGTH HAIR. THE FINE, JEWELED BRIDLE DRAWS ATTENTION TO THE MAN'S GLOVES, SILK JACKET, LEATHER COAT, FEATHERED HAT, FULL NECKPIECE AND THE WIDE BROCADED SASH THAT BINDS HIS WAIST, OVERFLOWING DOWN THE HORSE'S SIDE.

BEFORE THE AUTUMN-COLORED TREES ON THE LEFT, LIKE A DISTANT GLOWING EMBER, CAN BE SEEN A CARRIAGE WITH THREE FIGURES. AT THE UPPER RIGHT, LIKE A SPOTLIGHT BEHIND THE EQUESTRIAN'S HEAD, IS A HALF CIRCLE OF BLUE SKY AND TINTED CLOUD.

EQUESTRIAN PORTRAIT   THE NATIONAL GALLERY, LONDON, BY COURTESY OF THE TRUSTEES

IN THIS PAINTING, SASKIA AND REMBRANDT, THE ARTIST SHOWS HOW HE WAS LIVING AT THIS TIME OF HIS LIFE.

HE WAS THIRTY YEARS OLD, MARRIED INTO A GOOD FAMILY, FAMOUS, AND RAPIDLY BECOMING WEALTHY.

REMBRANDT BOUGHT FINE CLOTHES FOR HIS BRIDE OF ONE YEAR AND FOR HIMSELF.

HE FILLED THEIR HOME WITH BEAUTIFUL DRAPES, TABLECLOTHS, AND RARE PIECES OF FURNITURE.

HE BOUGHT ETCHINGS AND PAINTINGS BY OTHER WELL-KNOWN ARTISTS, OBJECTS OF ART LIKE THE SCULPTURED PEACOCK ON THE TABLE, SASKIA'S NECKLACE, THE LARGE WINEGLASS IN REMBRANDT'S RAISED HAND, AND HIS BRIGHT, SHINING SWORD.

FROM THE EXPRESSION ON HIS FACE, REMBRANDT SEEMS TO BE ENJOYING HIMSELF BUT SASKIA LOOKS AS THOUGH SHE DID NOT LIKE TO POSE.

SASKIA, 1633. DRAWING, BERLIN, PRINT ROOM

SASKIA AND REMBRANDT   STAATLICHE KUNSTSAMMLUNGEN , DRESDEN

TITUS WAS SASKIA AND REMBRANDT'S SON.
SOMETIMES PARENTS RELIVE THEIR OWN YOUTH IN THEIR
CHILDREN. IN THIS PORTRAIT WE CAN SEE REMBRANDT'S
IMAGE AS WELL AS HIS SON'S.

TITUS LOOKS UP FROM HIS WORK AND STUDIES THE
OBJECT HE IS DRAWING. HIS THUMB PRESSES HARD
AGAINST HIS CHIN IN CONCENTRATION. IT DIRECTS OUR
ATTENTION TO THE EYE DIRECTLY ABOVE THAT HAND.

THIS EYE, FULLY LIGHTED,
SEEMS TO RECORD VISUAL
LINES AND THE FORMS
THEY CREATE AS
ACCURATELY AS POSSIBLE.

THE OTHER EYE, IN SHADOW,
SEEMS TO SEARCH FOR
MEANINGS AND PURPOSE
IN THE FORMS.

SASKIA

TITUS' GOLDEN BROWN HAIR,
HIS HAND HOLDING THE INK-
WELL OVER THE EDGE OF
THE DESK, THE DRAWING
PAPER, HIS RED SHIRT AND
BERET ALL REMIND US
THAT THE ARTIST'S SON

MAY BE FOLLOWING THE PATH SET BY HIS FATHER.

TITUS AT A DESK   MUSEUM BOYMANS-VAN BEUNINGEN, ROTTERDAM

LANDSCAPE with OBELISK

IS ONE OF REMBRANDT'S FINEST
PORTRAITS OF NATURE.

BEGGAR LEANING ON A STICK,
RIJKSMUSEUM, AMSTERDAM

USING LIGHT AND SHADOW, THE ARTIST
SHOWS US THAT TREES, A RIVER, CLOUDS,
BUILDINGS, AND ANIMALS CAN HAVE
PERSONALITIES. WE RECOGNIZE EACH OF
THEM ON SIGHT, BUT HAVE TO SEARCH
OUR MINDS TO UNDERSTAND HOW
THEY AFFECT OUR LIVES.

REMBRANDT PAINTS YOUTH AND
OLD AGE IN HIS TREES. THERE ARE
STRETCHES OF CALM WATER ON THE RIVER AND PLACES
WHERE THERE ARE ROCKY FALLS.

GRAY AND WHITE CLOUDS MIX
TOGETHER IN THE SUN-TINTED BLUE
SKY. ONE DAY CAN HAVE MANY MOODS.

THIS LANDSCAPE WITH PEOPLE, HORSE,
BRIDGE, CART, WATER MILL, MONUMENT,
AND VILLAGE, ALL SEEN TOGETHER
UNDER THE BLUE HEAVENS, NOT
ONLY GIVES PLEASURE FOR OUR
EYES AS WE STUDY THE PAINTING,
BUT ALSO GIVES OUR MINDS A
GREAT DEAL TO THINK ABOUT. NATURE
CAN BE A GREAT TEACHER.

OLD BEGGAR WOMAN WITH A GOURD
NATIONAL GALLERY OF ART, WASHINGTON D.C., ROSENWALD COLLECTION

THE OBELISK   ISABELLA STEWART GARDNER MUSEUM, BOSTON

THE POLISH RIDER IS ONE OF REMBRANDT'S MOST EXCITING PAINTINGS.

EVERY DETAIL IS PAINTED WITH SUCH LOVING CARE THAT WE DO NOT KNOW WHERE TO LOOK FIRST.

THE FACE OF THE RIDER AND THE FACE OF THE HORSE ARE STUDIES IN CONTRASTING MOODS.

THE HORSE SURVEYS THE WAY BEFORE THEM, CAUTIOUSLY RAISING HIS FORELEG TO TEST HIS PATH.

THE MAN SEEMS TO BE LOST IN THOUGHT, BUT THE BODIES OF BOTH SPIRITED SUBJECTS ARE ERECT AND READY FOR ACTION.

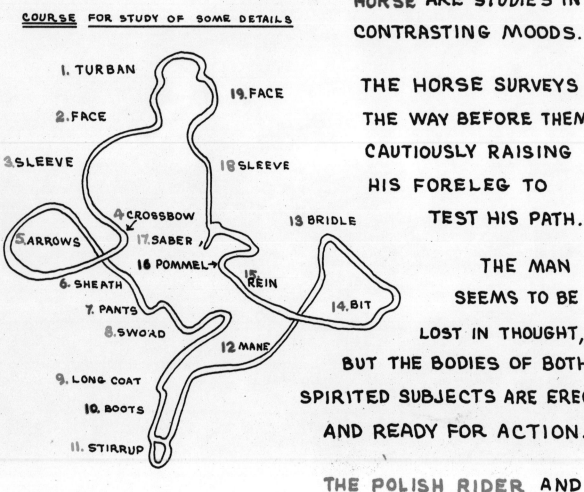

COURSE FOR STUDY OF SOME DETAILS

1. TURBAN
2. FACE
3. SLEEVE
4. CROSSBOW
5. ARROWS
6. SHEATH
7. PANTS
8. SWORD
9. LONG COAT
10. BOOTS
11. STIRRUP
12. MANE
13. BRIDLE
14. BIT
15. REIN
16. POMMEL →
17. SABER
18. SLEEVE
19. FACE

THE POLISH RIDER AND HIS HORSE ARE LIKE A PAINTED SCULPTURE CARVED IN MARBLE AND PLACED ON A MOUNTAIN LEDGE. REMBRANDT INVITES US TO SQUINT OUR EYES ―― AND IT SEEMS THAT THE HORSE AND RIDER ALMOST MOVE.

THE POLISH RIDER

HENDRICKJE STOFFELS STANDING AT HER WINDOW
IS A WARM, HAPPY PAINTING.

SHE IS REMBRANDT'S SECOND GREAT LOVE, THE
MOTHER OF HIS DAUGHTER CORNELIA.

THIS ARTIST, ONE OF THE GREATEST PORTRAIT PAINTERS
THE WORLD HAS EVER KNOWN, LET HIS HAND AND BRUSH
TELL AS TRUTHFULLY AS HE WAS ABLE WHAT HIS EYES
SAW ON A SUBJECT'S FACE.

REMBRANDT'S VISION WAS SUCH THAT HE WAS ABLE NOT
ONLY TO PAINT THE
OUTWARD APPEAR-
ANCE, THE PERSONALITY,
THE SPIRIT, AND
THE HIDDEN THOUGHTS,
BUT ALSO TO PUT
INTO EACH ONE OF
OVER 400 SUCH
PORTRAITS HIS OWN
PHILOSOPHY OF LIFE.

EVERY STROKE OF
HIS BRUSH WAS
A CARESS ON
THE SURFACE
OF THE PAINTING.

YOUNG WOMAN AT HER TOILET

HENDRICKJE STOFFELS   STAATLICHE MUSEUM, BERLIN (WEST)

THE MASTERS OF THE DRAPER'S GUILD IS ONE OF REMBRANDT'S COMMISSIONED PAINTINGS KNOWN AS "CORPORATION PORTRAITS."

IN THIS WORK THE ARTIST SHOWS HIS GENIUS FOR PUTTING A FEELING OF ACTION INTO A **STILL** PICTURE. IT IS AS IF WE HAD SUDDENLY WALKED INTO THIS MEETING AND SURPRISED THE MASTERS OF THE BOARD.

REMBRANDT HAD A SPECIAL RESPECT FOR THESE MEN. THEY WERE CRAFTSMEN LIKE HIMSELF. HIS UNDERSTANDING OF THEM LIGHTS EVERY FACE WITH INDIVIDUALITY.

THE PAINTER LIKED THESE HARD-WORKING MEN. PERHAPS WE WILL TOO IF WE STUDY EACH MEMBER CAREFULLY.

MASTERS OF THE DRAPER'S GUILD   RIJKSMUSEUM, AMSTERDAM

THE MILL STANDS, LIKE
A STRANGE FLYING
MACHINE, READY TO TAKE
OFF INTO THE SUNSET.

OVERHEAD, STORM CLOUDS ARE
MOVING OUT OF THE SKY.

THE WIND IS GONE. THE BLADES
OF THE WINDMILL STAND STILL.

THE BULL   RIJKSMUSEUM, AMSTERDAM

DOWN BELOW, ON THE QUIET WATER OF THE RIVER, A BOAT
WITH ITS LOWERED SAIL DRIFTS TOWARD THE BEACH AS
THE SKIPPER RESTS ON HIS OAR.

AWAITING HIS ARRIVAL, A GROUP OF VILLAGERS HAS GATHERED
NEAR THE
WATERFRONT.

THE DAY
IS
DONE.

IT IS
TIME
TO GO
HOME.

THE GOLF PLAYER   RIJKSMUSEUM, AMSTERDAM

THE MILL   NATIONAL GALLERY OF ART, WASHINGTON, D.C., WIDENER COLLECTION

HOMER DICTATING TO A YOUNG SCRIBE   DRAWING, NATIONAL MUSEUM, STOCKHOLM

ARISTOTLE CONTEMPLATING THE BUST OF HOMER IS
ONE OF THE MOST FAMOUS PAINTINGS IN THE WORLD.

REMBRANDT'S GLOWING GOLDEN STUDY SHOWS THE
FAMOUS GREEK PHILOSOPHER RESTING HIS HAND, AS THOUGH FOR
INSPIRATION, ON THE HEAD OF HIS COUNTRY'S BEST KNOWN POET,
HOMER.

THE GREEK PHILOSOPHERS PUT DOWN THEIR THOUGHTS IN COLORFUL
WORDS. THE DUTCH MASTER PAINTER WAS A PHILOSOPHER IN
COLORED PAINT, IN INK DRAWINGS, AND IN LINES ETCHED
ON COPPER PLATES.

REMBRANDT, ARISTOTLE, AND HOMER WERE ALL CONCERNED
WITH THE OBSERVATION OF THE NATURE OF MANKIND,
AND WITH TRUTH, BEAUTY, AND WISDOM.

ARISTOTLE CONTEMPLATING THE BUST OF HOMER   THE METROPOLITAN MUSEUM OF ART, NEW YORK

LANDSCAPE WITH WINDMILLS, WEST OF AMSTERDAM, 1655   THE ROYAL MUSEUM OF FINE ARTS, COPENHAGEN